Kirk Cousins: The Inspiring Story of One of Football's Star Quarterbacks

An Unauthorized Biography

By: Clayton Geoffreys

Copyright © 2023 by Calvintir Books, LLC

All rights reserved. Neither this book nor any portion thereof may be reproduced or used in any manner whatsoever without the express written permission. Published in the United States of America.

Disclaimer: The following book is for entertainment and informational purposes only. The information presented is without contract or any type of guarantee assurance. While every caution has been taken to provide accurate and current information, it is solely the reader's responsibility to check all information contained in this article before relying upon it. Neither the author nor publisher can be held accountable for any errors or omissions.

Under no circumstances will any legal responsibility or blame be held against the author or publisher for any reparation, damages, or monetary loss due to the information presented, either directly or indirectly. This book is not intended as legal or medical advice. If any such specialized advice is needed, seek a qualified individual for help.

Trademarks are used without permission. Use of the trademark is not authorized by, associated with, or sponsored by the trademark owners. All trademarks and brands used within this book are used with no intent to infringe on the trademark owners and only used for clarifying purposes.

This book is not sponsored by or affiliated with the National Football League, its teams, the players, or anyone involved with them.

Visit my website at www.claytongeoffreys.com
Cover photo by All-Pro Reels is licensed under CC BY-SA 2.0 / modified from original

Table of Contents

Foreword 1

Introduction 3

Chapter 1: Childhood & High School 17

Chapter 2: Michigan State 33

    The NFL Draft 52

Chapter 3: Pro Career 58

    Backup Again 58

    The Starter 67

    Up to the Great North 81

    COVID-19 88

Chapter 4: Personal Life 101

Chapter 5: Legacy 105

Final Word/About the Author 108

References 113

Foreword

Becoming a quarterback in the NFL is not easy. Kirk Cousins has had to work his way to becoming a starting quarterback. Drafted in the fourth round of the 2012 NFL Draft, Kirk was Robert Griffin III's backup for a few years before getting an opportunity to start due to RGIII's unfortunate injuries. Since those early years, Cousins has accomplished a lot, having been selected to four Pro Bowls in 2016, 2019, 2021 and 2022. In 2015, he led the league in completion percentage. Thank you for purchasing *Kirk Cousins: The Inspiring Story of One of Football's Star Quarterbacks*. In this unauthorized biography, we will learn Kirk Cousins' incredible life story and impact on the game of football. Hope you enjoy and if you do, please do not forget to leave a review!

Also, check out my website at claytongeoffreys.com to join my exclusive list where I let you know about my latest books. To thank you for your purchase, you can go to my site to download a free copy of *33 Life Lessons: Success Principles, Career Advice & Habits of Successful People.* In the book, you'll learn from some of the greatest thought leaders of different industries on what it takes to become successful and how to live a great life.

Cheers,

Clayton Geoffreys

Visit me at www.claytongeoffreys.com

Introduction

In football, everyone's favorite player on the team when things aren't going well is the backup quarterback. The quarterback throws an interception, and the fans scream for the backup. If the team starts losing games, the fans want the coach to shake things up by bringing in the backup.

It rarely ever works, though. Coaches know that backup quarterbacks are that way for a reason. Perhaps they do not have the skills or experience to be a starter in the league yet, or maybe their prime years are largely behind them. But none of that matters to fans. All they see is what is in front of them on the field, and that product is not good enough when their beloved team is struggling.

This illogical yet somehow irresistible impulse of fans often leads them to speculate that they may have the next great quarterback sitting on the bench. How will they know if the next Tom Brady is holding a table on the sideline if he never gets a chance to play? And to be fair, there have been occasions when the backup *did* go on to enjoy great success.

Of course, Tom Brady is the story that fans always gravitate to, not the dozens of other backups who failed. Fans want to believe that they have the guy to lead them to the Super Bowl. But while Brady is the ultimate example of a backup quarterback that is most frequently cited, there were others who succeeded as well. Aaron Rodgers spent the first three seasons of his career as the backup to Brett Favre before he finally got a chance in year four, ultimately leading the Packers to a Super Bowl win.

Backup Kurt Warner took over the Rams after starting quarterback Trent Green blew out his knee in a preseason game. Warner went on to win a Super Bowl and became a Hall-of-Fame quarterback.

Steve Young, originally the backup to Hall-of-Famer Joe Montana, did the same thing with the 49ers. When

Young got the chance to start, he won a Super Bowl and ended up in the Hall of Fame himself.

Frank Reich took over the helm for the Buffalo Bills in the playoffs. He led Buffalo back from a 32-point deficit against the Houston Oilers in the Divisional Round. It was the largest comeback in the history of the NFL. Reich then traveled to Pittsburgh the next week and beat the Steelers 24-3. Yet, starter Jim Kelly returned the following week for another Buffalo Super Bowl loss.

Sure, all those stories are great, but in most cases, the truth is that the backup quarterback usually fails—but this book isn't about them. Instead, this is the story of a backup quarterback who came off that bench and triumphed.

Kirk Cousins was a backup everywhere he went. It started when he was at Michigan State, where he had to sit behind starter Brian Hoyer. It happened to him again when he was drafted by Washington and had to sit behind starter and former Heisman Trophy winner Robert Griffin III.

But each time he was forced to sit, Cousins learned and continued to get better until his number was finally called.

Cousins was born in Illinois but later moved to Michigan. His father was the team chaplain for the Chicago Bears. When Cousins first started playing football, his coach was Hall-of-Fame linebacker Mike Singletary.

When Cousins was 18 months old, he accidentally spilled a pot of boiling water on himself. The doctors told his parents that he might not have full range of motion in his right arm as a result of the accident. Cousins spent two weeks in the hospital, and through his hard work and dedication, he was eventually able to overcome the injury to throw a football.

Once he recovered from his injuries, Cousins headed outside to play with his older brother, Kyle. The two

Cousins boys were inseparable as children. They also had a fierce competitive streak in them that boiled over into all the games they played. Nearly every day, one of them would come into the house complaining about having lost the game they were playing outside.

When Cousins finally got on the football field, his father was his head coach, and Mike Singletary was his defensive coordinator. Little did he know that Singletary would get the chance to coach Cousins again in the Senior Bowl. Cousins' dad let his son air the ball out, unlike other teams that relied on the run.

When Kirk was 13, the family moved from Illinois to Michigan. He continued to play football, basketball, and baseball in Michigan, but he refused to become a Detroit sports fan. He stayed true to his Bears and Bulls.

Cousins enrolled at Holland Christian High School in Holland, Michigan. His first varsity playing time actually came in baseball, not football. But at the start of his junior season, he was finally the starting varsity quarterback. Unfortunately, during the first game of his junior season, he broke his ankle, costing him the entire season.

Without a junior year of accomplishments to show to colleges, Kirk had to attend camps and showcases to market his skills. All of the college coaches were impressed with his arm strength, but they did not like his measurables. He only ran the 40-yard dash in five seconds.

Kirk finally got his opportunity to start during his senior year and had a solid season, but still no FBS scholarship offers. Finally, during basketball season, he received offers from Toledo and Western Michigan.

Meanwhile, miles away in East Lansing, Michigan State University had just hired a new football coach, Mark Dantonio. When he was hired, Dantonio's quarterback recruit withdrew to attend another school.

Dantonio then offered for five other quarterbacks before he finally landed on Cousins.

Despite needing a quarterback, Dantonio was not convinced that Cousins was his man. Cousins came to Michigan State on a recruiting trip, more to sell himself than for the university to sell him. Dantonio was impressed with his maturity and poise. Nevertheless, after sending an assistant coach to watch Cousins' practice—interestingly, it was a *basketball* practice—he offered him a football scholarship.

Cousins was now on his way to play for the Spartans at Michigan State.

When Cousins arrived on campus, he was sitting behind starting quarterback Brian Hoyer. Despite not being known for producing quarterbacks, Michigan State's roster had three future NFL starters: Cousins, Hoyer, and future Eagles' Super Bowl MVP Nick Foles. Foles was a freshman along with Cousins and would later transfer to Arizona.

Cousins redshirted for his first year on campus and sat behind Hoyer his second year. In his redshirt sophomore year, he won the starting job. The Spartans went 6-6 in the regular season but lost the Alamo Bowl to Texas Tech.

During his redshirt junior year, Cousins and the Spartans started to come into their own. Michigan State finished the regular season at 11-1 and won a share of the Big Ten title. However, an October loss at Iowa cost them a shot at a national championship. Then, in the Citrus Bowl on New Year's Day, the Spartans were blown out by the defending national champion, Alabama. Their 11 wins were tied for the most in school history and they ended the year ranked 14th.

Despite having two solid seasons as a starter, Cousins was not receiving much attention heading into his final season at Michigan State. He was viewed by most scouts as a solid "game manager."

Michigan State had another good year in Cousins' senior season. They won the Big Ten East title and took on Wisconsin in the championship game. But after having beaten the Badgers in a thrilling October game, the Spartans fell by a mere field goal in the championship game.

In his last career college game, Cousins and the Spartans beat Georgia in the Outback Bowl in a three-overtime thriller. Cousins left Michigan State as the school's all-time leader in passing yards and touchdowns. He was the only quarterback in school history to beat Michigan three times in a row.

Cousins was selected in the fourth round of the NFL draft by the Washington Redskins. Washington had already used a pick that draft on a quarterback, selecting Heisman Trophy winner Robert Griffin III out of Baylor with the second-overall pick.

So, once again, Kirk Cousins was a backup quarterback. But Griffin was a running quarterback and was frequently injured in his rookie season. Cousins played sparingly for most of the season but started Week 15 against Cleveland. He had his first career 300-yard and two-touchdown game in a victory over the Browns.

Washington won the NFC East and took on Seattle in the Wild Card round of the playoffs that year. Cousins had to come into the game after Griffin tore his ACL in the game. Seattle dominated the game, ending Washington's season.

In his second and third seasons, Cousins remained the backup for most of the season. He got sporadic starts when Griffin was hurt.

But by his fourth season, Cousins won the starting quarterback job from Griffin. In a win over Tampa Bay, Cousins ran off the field, looked into a camera, and yelled, "You like that" at a sports reporter. The phrase would become his slogan, and he started selling t-shirts with the slogan on them to benefit the International Justice Mission.

In his first season as a starter, Kirk Cousins threw for more than 4,000 yards and led Washington to the playoffs. He set Washington's single-season passing yards record and led the NFL in completion percentage as well.

In the playoffs, despite Cousins throwing for more than 300 yards and two touchdowns, Washington still lost to Green Bay. Cousins was sacked six times in the game and lost a fumble.

In his final two seasons in Washington, Cousins threw for more than 4,000 yards and was named to his first Pro Bowl. But Washington missed the playoffs both years.

Cousins and the Redskins were not able to come to a contract agreement, and he subsequently signed a three-year, $84-million, fully-guaranteed contract with Minnesota. In his first season with the Vikings,

Cousins faced a win-or-go-home final game for the second time in three seasons. And for the second time in three seasons, his team lost the game.

With his team constantly losing late-season games, Kirk Cousins was developing an unfortunate reputation as a quarterback who came up small in the big spots. By the end of his first season in Minnesota, Cousins was 0-9 in prime-time games.

In 2019, Cousins was finally able to get his first playoff win in the Wild Card round against the Saints. But the thrill of victory was short-lived, as the Vikings were eliminated from the playoffs the following week by the 49ers.

During the COVID-19 season, controversy found Cousins because he did not strictly follow the NFL's protocols for COVID-19. Despite the controversy, Cousins had another successful season. He won his first-ever *Monday Night Football* game, but the Vikings *still* did not make the playoffs.

In 2021, controversy followed Cousins again, as he did not receive his COVID-19 vaccine and was placed on the NFL's COVID-19 list, which forced him to miss part of training camp. In the second-to-last week of the season, Cousins contracted COVID-19 and was forced to miss a game against the Packers. Minnesota lost the game, which eliminated them from the playoffs.

Cousins had his most successful season in 2022. He led Minnesota to its first NFC North title with him as the quarterback. The Vikings won 13 games, which was the most wins for Cousins in his career. He was named to his fourth Pro Bowl and led eight game-winning drives, which was the most in NFL history.

Yet, despite all his and the Vikings' accomplishments in 2022, they were eliminated by the New York Giants in the Wild Card Round of the playoffs. In his career, Cousins is 1-3 in the playoffs.

Kirk Cousins has been one of the most consistent quarterbacks in the NFL over his eight seasons as a starter. However, team success in the playoffs continues to elude him, and his critics continue to point to his lack of big-game wins. But for a fourth-round pick, Kirk Cousins has gone further than anyone ever expected. From backup to reliable starter, he's been a surprise, and perhaps his best accomplishments are yet to come.

Chapter 1: Childhood & High School

The Midwest is the cradle of professional football. The 10-team NFL (originally called the APFA, or *American Professional Football Association*) was founded in Canton, Ohio, and spread across Ohio, Michigan, Indiana, and Illinois. In 1920, the Chicago Cardinals hosted the Decatur Staleys. This would become the oldest rivalry in the NFL. Eventually, the Staleys would move to Chicago and change their names to the Bears, thanks to owner/coach George Halas.

By the late 1980s, the Bears were one of the most dominant teams in the history of the NFL. Chicago won eight NFL championships and in 1986, won its first Super Bowl. Two years later, future Bear fan Kirk Cousins was born.

Kirk Cousins was born on August 19, 1988, to Don and Maryann Cousins in Barrington, Illinois. Don was the Chicago Bears' team chaplain and was good friends with Hall-of-Fame linebackers Mike Singletary and Leslie Frazier. Don was with the Bears when they won their first Super Bowl against the New England Patriots.

Both Frazier and Singletary would go into coaching after their playing careers finished, and both would eventually become head coaches in the NFL. Frazier would coach the Minnesota Vikings for three and a half seasons, and Singletary would spend two and a half seasons as the head coach of the San Francisco 49ers.

Kirk was the middle child of three. An accident when he was just a toddler would nearly end any hopes of playing sports, and also nearly ended his life. With three kids, Maryann lost track of 18-month-old Kirk. Without his mother's watchful eye, Kirk accidentally poured a pot of boiling water on himself.

"There were a lot of injuries," Kirk said. "I was in the hospital for two weeks. One of the things the doctor said was that you may never get a full range of motion in your shoulders. To be out here, playing football and throwing the football, it's kind of a neat thing to be able to have overcome that."[i]

That injury could have easily prevented Kirk's football career, but even at such a young age, he worked hard and overcame the pain. Hurting himself and still being able to play sports would be a lesson that helped define Kirk for the remainder of his life. Despite future setbacks and injuries, he would never count himself out.

But Kirk was not alone in his battle, nor would he ever be. The Cousins family was a tight unit, and they overcame obstacles together. With Kirk's father being a pastor, religion played an important role in Kirk's life as well as in the lives of his family. The family also included Kirk's grandparents who lived 20 minutes away, but the family would gather every Sunday for church, followed by dinner.

Kirk also had his older brother, Kyle, as a motivator. The brothers were only 22 months apart and did everything together when they were growing up. There was also a friendly rivalry between the two because they were so close in age.

"It was very, very competitive, but in the context of being brothers," Kyle said. "It was a healthy competition. Like any brothers, we got into our battles."[ii]

At first, Kyle had the upper hand over his younger brother, but no matter what happened, Kirk competed hard against his brother.

"They've always competed with each other—in the backyard, in the driveway," Don said. "Kyle was always a little faster and a little stronger than Kirk. But Kirk always battled and competed. He didn't whine, sulk, or complain because he was losing."[iii]

The brothers played various sports by the season. Football in the fall, basketball in the winter, and baseball in the spring and summer. Eventually, Kirk would overtake his older brother and take over as the quarterback during backyard football games. He soon began to show the arm strength that would eventually get him into the NFL. But even though he was starting to become the superior athlete, Kirk never let his older brother miss out on the spotlight.

"There was a game playing flag football together," Kyle said. "I was receiver. He was quarterback. I was going to go deep on a fly. I remember I dropped it, the first try. I was upset. Kirk had thrown a perfect spiral. Two or three plays later, he came back to me, and I caught it for a touchdown. It felt so good because we scored."[iv]

Growing up just outside of Chicago and having a father who worked for the team, Kirk was a die-hard Bears fan as a kid. So, it was a special treat when Bears legend Mike Singletary joined the coaching staff of Kirk's Pee Wee football team.

For two seasons, Singletary coached the defense while Kirk's father, Don, coached the offense. Singletary's son, Matt, was Kirk's teammate. It would be Singletary who taught Kirk how to tackle.

"It was unique," Kirk said. "A lot of parents would come to the games and bring memorabilia to have signed. A lot of parents wanted their kids to be on his team. He would bring dummies to practice and demonstrate the drills with perfect form. I don't think the other dads in the league coaching were providing the same level of expertise."[v]

Singletary brought the same intensity to coaching Kirk and the other kids in Pee Wee that he would later bring to coaching the 49ers. However, he did not really know that much about the offense the team was running. During one game when Don could not be there, Singletary acted as both the head coach and offensive coordinator. Instead of calling plays himself, he let Kirk call the offense, and their team won the game.

At the time, most of the offenses young kids ran were run-based, but with Kirk being able to throw the ball all over the field, Don let his son air it out, and that was exactly what Kirk did. Despite lacking the prototypical physical numbers of a future-NFL quarterback, he always had a strong arm and was able to throw a perfect spiral every time.

"At that age, the kids are so young that you don't know how good they will be," Singletary said. "But Kirk was very focused. He was intense and he was very goal oriented. If you told him to do something, he wanted to do it right. I didn't know that he was going to use that focus to play football or do something else, but I knew there was a good chance he was going to be successful."[vi]

When Kirk was 13, the Cousins family moved from Illinois to Michigan. Unlike most kids, who would be worried about leaving their home or their friends, Kirk was more worried about leaving his teams behind.

"I remember when we left Illinois for Michigan, I said, 'Dad, does this mean we have to become Lions and Pistons and fans of the state of Michigan and Detroit?'" Kirk said. "He said, 'Kirk, you can take the boy out of Chicago. You can't take the Chicago out of the boy.' We stayed Chicago sports fans when we moved to Michigan, and where we were in the state was actually probably closer to Chicago than Detroit anyway, so we could justify it that way as well. Unfortunately, right when we moved, the Pistons won the championship, so I had to hear it from all my friends. Naturally, all those teams were on TV, so I saw a lot of the Lions through the years."[vii]

Nevertheless, Kirk, Kyle, and Don would frequently make it back to Chicago to attend Bears games.

Kirk enrolled at Holland Christian High School in Holland, Michigan. At first, it appeared as though baseball might be his path to stardom. As a freshman and sophomore at the school, Kirk only played junior varsity football but played some varsity games in baseball during his sophomore season. He split time between pitching and playing third base.

It was while he was in high school that Kirk picked up another one of his favorite hobbies, reading. He had always kept a copy of the Bible with him, but now that he was in high school, Kirk expanded his repertoire of books, including his favorite, CS Lewis' *The Screwtape Letters*.

Despite being a star athlete in high school, Kirk remained humble and kind. One day, his AP Literature teacher, Mark Hiskes, mentioned that his wife was in Ghana with a Christian medical aid organization. Kirk grew concerned that his teacher might have to eat dinner alone, so he asked his teacher if he wanted to come over for a cookout that weekend.

"That was a cool idea, but then I thought, 'Well, I'm not sure I want to spend a whole night with two high school guys,'" Hiskes said.[viii]

So, to help alleviate Hiskes' concerns, Kirk invited every guy in the senior class and every senior male teacher. The cookouts that Kirk organized continued regularly for the next four or five years.

"I knew when he went into football, but, particularly the NFL, I said, 'This guy's going to change the NFL before the NFL's going to change him.'" Hiskes said.[ix]

When Cousins arrived at Holland Christian High School, the football program had just started playing. The team was so new that Kyle had to play soccer when he first arrived at the school, as it was the only fall sport Holland offered. So, the school was not exactly a hotbed for recruiting, nor did it yet have the kind of staff that could easily get kids into colleges. To get his name out there, Kirk started attending camps and clinics.

Prior to his junior season, Kirk attended a camp at Purdue University. There, his throwing ability caught the eye of quarterback guru Bob Johnson, who desperately tried to get Purdue to recruit him. But because Kirk lacked the measurables of a prototypical quarterback, Purdue passed on him.

"Just about everywhere I went, I threw the ball well enough to where they were interested and they were going to keep tabs on me," Kirk said. "But I didn't run a fast enough 40, or I wasn't big enough."[x]

Finally, during his junior season, Kirk got his chance to show what he could do on the field for Holland Christian. Unfortunately, Kirk broke his ankle during the first game of his junior season, costing him the remainder of the year.

Kirk was devasted heading home from the doctor's office after he was told that his entire junior season would be lost. But Don Cousins reminded his son of the family's favorite Bible passage, Proverbs 3:5-6, which read: "Trust in the Lord with all your heart and lean not on your own understanding. In all your ways submit to him, and he will make your paths straight." The verse would become Kirk's motto for the rest of his life.

The summer before his senior season, Kirk headed back to the camp circuit, hoping to impress a coach enough to get a scholarship offer. But, with no game tape to show the coaches, the offers he hoped to receive just did not come.

"Going into your senior year, most big-time schools have already gotten their quarterback," Kirk said. "You're looking at going to a MAC school, probably. And that's what I was hoping for. I was hoping for a Western Michigan or a Toledo to come in if I had a good season."[xi]

The issue that Kirk kept having was that when coaches looked at his arm, they were impressed, but then they looked at his numbers and weren't that impressed. He was 6'2" but only weighed 160 pounds heading into his senior season. He also ran a 5.0 in the 40-yard dash. That was a good time for an offensive lineman, but not for a quarterback.

When the time finally came for Kirk to step onto the field, he played well for Holland Christian. He ended his senior season with 3,204 yards and 40 touchdowns. But even when the season was over, he still did not have a scholarship offer from an FBS school.

Finally, the two-star recruit received two scholarship offers during basketball season. Western Michigan and Toledo both offered Kirk a football scholarship. But Kirk had big dreams, and neither of those schools was ideal for him.

"I couldn't see myself there," was how Kirk described the two scholarship offers from the MAC schools.[xii]

Meanwhile, a few miles away in East Lansing, Michigan, something was happening that Kirk had nothing to do with and no control over, but it would change his life forever.

Michigan State University had hired Mark Dantonio to be its head football coach. Dantonio just left the University of Cincinnati after a successful run with the Bearcats. When the previous staff was fired, the team's top-recruited quarterback decided to de-commit from the Spartans and attend another school. This happens quite frequently when a new coaching staff is hired because they want to bring in players who can fit their system.

But now, Dantonio had an opening for a quarterback. So, he started recruiting every quarterback who had not signed with another school. He ultimately landed on Matt Simms, son of former Super Bowl MVP Phil Simms. However, Simms decided to sign with Louisville. So, Dantonio went on to option two, then three, and eventually four.

"I was like option six," Kirk said. "And options one through five went elsewhere."[xiii]

In January of his senior year, Kirk made an official visit to Michigan State. He was the only player there who did not have a scholarship offer from the school. He went to convince the Michigan State coaching staff that they should take a chance on him.

"I went on the official visit trying to woo them to offer me," Kirk said. "You just try to look them in the eye, shake their hand. If you don't run a 4.5, if you don't weigh 210 pounds, you show them that as a person, you're going to be someone they want. You just try to be a stand-up person."[xiv]

Dantonio was impressed with the person, but he still was not sure about the football player. He sent assistant coach Don Treadwell to watch Kirk's basketball practice, of all things. Treadwell came back impressed, not just with Kirk's athletic ability but also his leadership skills. A few days later, Michigan State offered Kirk Cousins a scholarship to play football for the Spartans.

"He doesn't have to just be a great quarterback," Dantonio said. "He's going to be a great husband, a great father, a great community leader. The guy just sort of has it as a person."[xv]

With only one option, Kirk Cousins accepted his scholarship offer and was on his way to East Lansing.

Chapter 2: Michigan State

Michigan State is not exactly known for producing great quarterbacks. It doesn't nearly have the reputation of USC or Miami. Prior to Kirk Cousins' arrival on campus, the best quarterback the school had ever produced was probably Earl Morrall, who was the starting quarterback for the Indianapolis Colts in Super Bowl III against the New York Jets. Morrall was eventually replaced in the game by Hall-of-Famer Johnny Unitas. Later in life, Colts' Coach Don Shula said that he had waited too long to replace Morrall with Unitas, which was why the Colts lost to the improbable Jets.

When Cousins arrived at Michigan State in 2007, the Spartans would have three future starting NFL quarterbacks in their locker room. There was, of course, Cousins, who would be a future starter for Washington and Minnesota. Meanwhile, the starting quarterback when Cousins arrived on campus was

Brian Hoyer. Hoyer would eventually win a Super Bowl as Tom Brady's backup in New England and become a starter in Cleveland. The third future starting NFL quarterback was freshman Nick Foles. Foles arrived on campus with Cousins but soon transferred to Arizona. Foles would win a Super Bowl MVP while playing for Philadelphia.

Cousins was already at a disadvantage when he arrived in East Lansing. Having been recruited so late in the process, he did not have time to start learning Michigan State's new offense or to start working out with his new teammates. On top of that, Cousins got there two weeks late for the start of fall practice. He had been on a religious trip to Israel that delayed his reporting to campus.

As a result, Cousins would redshirt for his first year with the Spartans and lead the scout team offense against Michigan State's starting defense. Cousins and the rest of the scout team took a daily beating against the Spartans' defense, but that did not matter to him. He began to show his leadership abilities in those scout team practices.

"I could definitely tell he was going to be a leader," Guard Joel Foreman said. "Right off the bat, he was the leader of our class. He was the guy you looked up to. Anything you needed, you went to Kirk. It was no surprise two years later when he was the captain of the team."[xvi]

Michigan State finished the 2007 season at 7-6 after losing to Boston College in the Champs Sports Bowl. In Dantonio's first season, the Spartans went 3-5 in Big Ten play.

"I knew I wasn't good enough, yet." Cousins said. "I wasn't okay with sitting on the bench for five years. I wanted to make sure that I was going to be good enough to play someday. What kept me motivated was the fact that I wasn't there yet, and I had a lot of work to do. I wanted to put the work in so that I would be able to play someday."[xvii]

When Cousins returned for his sophomore season, Hoyer was still the starter, and he was going to have to watch from the bench. After losing to Cal on the road, the Spartans returned home to face Eastern Michigan. With the win firmly in place, Cousins saw his first college action. He went 3-4 for 34 yards in his first time on the field. Nothing spectacular, but it would be the first of many completions for Cousins at Michigan State.

The Spartans won their next seven games and rose all the way to number 20 in the rankings. In Week 8, Michigan State hosted Number 12 Ohio State in the Spartans' first true test of the season. Late in the first half, Hoyer took a hit but stayed in the game. Yet, when the teams returned to the field for halftime, Hoyer remained in the locker room.

Down 28-0, Cousins was going to get his first test in college. He led the Spartans right down the field on an 85-yard drive for their first touchdown of the game. It appeared Cousins was about to show some of that magic that he would later be famous for.

The Michigan State defense held Ohio State, but on the next play, Cousins was sacked. The ball squirted out, and Ohio State's Thaddeus Gibson scooped up the fumble and took it 69 yards for a touchdown. That ended any hopes the Spartans had of a comeback.

"We were working to at least try and be respectable," Dantonio said. "You can't snap your fingers and say, 'It's 28-all.' You have to claw your way back. If we could've gotten to 14 and been down 14, the whole complexion of the sideline changes."[xviii]

Cousins also saw time in Michigan State's final game of the season, a blowout loss to Penn State. He would throw his second touchdown pass of the season.

In the Citrus Bowl, Michigan State took on Georgia in a New Year's Day bowl game. With the Spartan offense struggling in the first half, Dantonio benched Hoyer and put Cousins in the game. It ultimately did not help, as Matthew Stafford threw three touchdown passes in the second half to lead Georgia to the 24-12 victory.

That would be Hoyer's last game at Michigan State, however. He went undrafted but was picked up by the Patriots and spent the first part of his career with New England. Michigan State was now Kirk Cousins' team.

Just before the season started, and despite not having started a single game, the Michigan State players voted Kirk Cousins one of their team captains.

"It was humbling and an honor," Cousins said. "I was thankful to my teammates for the opportunity they gave me. I wanted to make sure I led at a high level all season and tried to do that. It's a great opportunity to try and make a difference and be a leader, not only on this football team, but on this campus. I try to impact people in the right way, for the right things."[xix]

Cousins started his first game for Michigan State against FCS Montana State. He would end the game with 183 yards and 3 touchdowns in his first career win.

"When I started my first game, that was a dream come true," Cousins said. "I knew there was still a lot of work to be done. And I think that is kind of the mentality whenever you accomplish something, you're always looking at the next thing to accomplish. It was a special accomplishment and a day I will always remember."[xx]

It would be a while before Cousins felt good about football. Michigan State would go on to lose its next three games, and all by narrow margins. In the second game at Notre Dame, Cousins threw an interception with 50 seconds remaining in the Fighting Irish's end zone to seal the victory for Notre Dame. The Spartans lost the game by three points. The Spartans would lose those three games by a combined total of just 13 points.

The following week, 1-3 Michigan State hosted their archrival, Michigan, who came into the game undefeated and ranked 22 in the country. The two teams met early for the Paul Bunyan Trophy.

With the Spartans up by two touchdowns late in the game, Cousins was forced to leave the game with an ankle injury. He watched from the sideline as Michigan came all the way back in the final four minutes of the game to tie the score. In overtime, Michigan State intercepted a Michigan pass and scored a rushing touchdown to win the game by six.

It was Michigan State's second straight win over the Wolverines, and it was the first time that they beat their rivals in back-to-back seasons in 42 years.

Cousins' ankle injury was so bad that he was forced to miss the following week against Illinois, a 24-14 victory. But two weeks later, Cousins was back under center, and the Spartans were hosting Number 6 and undefeated Iowa. With 1:37 remaining, Cousins threw a touchdown pass to put Michigan State up 13-9. Iowa was able to drive the ball down the field and scored as time expired to win the game, 15-13. It was a heartbreaking loss for the Spartans.

After a loss at Minnesota, Cousins had the best game of his career against Western Michigan. He threw for 353 yards and 2 touchdowns in a 49-14 win.

The Spartans ended the regular season at 6-6, good enough to earn a trip to the Alamo Bowl in San Antonio, Texas. Nine of Michigan State's players were suspended for the game and were facing misdemeanor assault charges stemming from a fight. Despite missing so many players, the Spartans still had the lead late in the fourth quarter but were outscored 13-0 in the game's final five minutes, leading to a Texas Tech victory. Michigan State finished the season 6-7.

"I think the important thing about losing is to nail and press on," Cousins said. "You have to learn from your mistakes but not dwell on them. It's important to make sure that you're constantly looking to improve but also focusing on the positives. Stay positive. I think especially as a leader, it is important to stay positive."[xxi]

In his first season as a starter, Cousins had a solid season. He threw for 2,680 yards and 19 touchdowns in 12 games. It was a good, but not great, season for Cousins.

Entering the 2010 season, Cousins was more prepared for the rigors of a college football season. He was once again voted Captain of the Michigan State football team, and his confidence was up.

"There was a lot more confidence going into 2010 because I had been there before," Cousins said. "We didn't have as good of a season in 2009, going 6-7, but we learned a lot and there was no substitute for that experience. I think that showed in 2010 when we won

11 games and won the Big Ten title. It was a special season from start to finish. It was a tremendous way to end the year at Penn State with a Big Ten title."[xxii]

Michigan State also added a new weapon for Cousins in freshman running back Le'Veon Bell. Bell would help take some of the pressure off of Cousins. The future Steeler All-Pro became the first Michigan State running back to rush for more than 100 yards in his first-ever game.

After two easy wins, the Spartans hosted Notre Dame. Cousins threw two touchdown passes, including one in the fourth quarter to tie the score. In overtime, Notre Dame got the ball first and kicked a field goal. On Michigan State's possession, the Spartans lined up for a field goal, but Dantonio called a fake. The Spartans executed the play for a game-winning touchdown. It was sweet revenge after the three-point loss the previous season.

After the game, Dantonio suffered a mild heart attack. He was forced to miss the next two games but would return in Week 6 at Michigan. For the third straight season, Michigan State knocked off their rivals for the Paul Bunyan Trophy. This time it was in convincing fashion.

The Spartans were 8-0 heading into Iowa to play the 18th-ranked Hawkeyes. Michigan State had moved all the way up to eight in the polls after being unranked to start the season. Cousins was awful in the game. He threw three interceptions, and Michigan State did not see the end zone until the fourth quarter, and by then, the game was over.

"If you look at Iowa today, we ran into a buzzsaw. Where they come off a loss and you could tell, they said, 'We're not going to lose today. We're not going to lose at home, we're not going to lose two in a row,'" Cousins said.[xxiii]

Michigan State just missed out on being 9-0 for the first time since they won the National Championship in 1966. But there was still hope for a Big 10 title if they won the remainder of their games. And that's what they did.

The Spartans would win the final two games of their season and secure the Big 10 title. Their 11 wins in the regular season were tied for the most in school history. They earned a trip to the Capital One Bowl on New Year's Day to take on national powerhouse Alabama.

The Crimson Tide were the defending national champions but lost a heartbreaker in the Iron Bowl to Auburn, costing them another shot at a title. Alabama's starting 22 would have 13 future NFL players on it.

Alabama ran all over Michigan State. The Tide scored four rushing touchdowns in the first half, putting the game away. Cousins spent most of the game running for his life. He was sacked five times and hit nearly three times as many. He left the game in the fourth quarter with a headache, but the game was already out of reach for the Spartans.

For Cousins, it was a successful season. He led the Spartans to 11 wins while throwing for 2,825 yards and 20 touchdowns. Even his biggest fan thought so.

"This season has been a joy for me to see Kirk enjoying the rewards of all the hard work he put in," Kyle Cousins, Kirk's brother, said. "Last year was a very frustrating situation. There were a lot of the games that could have gone our way that didn't. To see games like Purdue and Northwestern where Kirk takes the reins and brings the team back into the game—not single-handedly—I've been seeing him do that since we were kids. To see him on this kind of a stage is a joy. Joy is probably an understatement."[xxiv]

Cousins entered his fifth and final season at Michigan State looking to repeat as Big Ten champions and finally win a bowl game as a starter. The Spartans won their first two games easily and then headed to Notre Dame.

It was all Fighting Irish. Cousins threw a career-high 53 passes, but it was only because Notre Dame opened an early lead and the Spartans were playing from behind all game long.

After beating Central Michigan, the Spartans had to run the Big Ten gauntlet. They would face Ohio State, Michigan, and Wisconsin in three consecutive weeks. The first challenge was a trip to Columbus to take on the Buckeyes. Cousins threw a touchdown pass in the first quarter, and it would be the only touchdown in the game until there were only 10 seconds remaining. Michigan State escaped with a 10-7 win over the Buckeyes.

The following week, the Spartans hosted Number 11, an undefeated Michigan. Cousins threw two touchdown passes, and the Michigan State defense scored a touchdown in the Spartans 28-14 win.

Cousins became the first quarterback in school history to win three games against rival Michigan.

The final team in the gauntlet was undefeated, fourth-ranked Wisconsin. Cousins threw three touchdown passes in the game, but none was more impressive than the last one. With the game tied at 31, the Spartans had time for one last play. Cousins heaved the ball to the end zone from 44 yards away, connecting with Keith Nichol for the game-winning touchdown.

"We knew we had a chance," Cousins said. "There's always a chance."[xxv]

After the thrilling high of a game-winning Hail Mary, Cousins and the Spartans hit the low point of their season the following week at Number 13 Nebraska. Cousins had his worst game as a college quarterback. He only completed 11 passes and threw an interception in Michigan State's 24-3 loss.

"We're a much better team than we showed today, and we still have a lot of things in front of us to accomplish," Cousins said. "It's important to push on and understand that so much of what happens to us this season is not what happened to us but how we respond. It's important that we respond the right way."[xxvi]

Michigan State rebounded to win its final four Big Ten games and earn a trip to the inaugural Big Ten championship game. Waiting for them would be Wisconsin, whom the Spartans only beat on a Hail Mary. The winner of this game would earn a trip to the Rose Bowl.

The Spartans moved the ball at will against the Wisconsin defense, outscoring them 22-0 in the second quarter. With 3:45 left in the game, the Badgers scored the game-winning touchdown, taking the Big Ten championship and the trip to the Rose Bowl.

"We felt we were having our way offensively the whole game," Cousins said. "We never felt like it was won. But we felt like we had our way offensively. It's tough. We came close two years in a row. We don't get to go, it's tough."xxvii

As a consolation prize, Michigan State was invited to take on Georgia in the Outback Bowl on New Year's Day. The Bulldogs opened up a 16-0 halftime lead, and it appeared as though Cousins was going to leave college without a bowl win.

The Spartans started chipping away in the third quarter, but with less than two minutes remaining, Michigan State was still down by seven. Cousins led the team down the field for the game-tying touchdown with less than 20 seconds remaining, sending the game into overtime.

Neither team scored in the first overtime and traded field goals in the second overtime. Finally, in the third overtime, the Michigan State defense forced Georgia into a missed field goal, and Michigan State kicked a 28-yard field goal for the win. Cousins had won his first bowl game by throwing for 300 yards and a touchdown.

"And at halftime we had our doubts because of how successful their defense was in stopping us. But we found a way. It wasn't perfect, but we certainly showed character, and that's what I'm most proud of," Cousins said after the game. "We played with a great deal of maturity and toughness, and we weren't afraid. We didn't back down, and we found a way at the end. And that's what great teams do."[xxviii]

Besides being Cousins' first bowl victory, it was also Dantonio's first bowl victory with the Spartans.

Cousins would leave Michigan State as the team's all-time leader in passing yards and touchdowns. Both of his records would be broken by Connor Cook, who took over at quarterback after Cousins left for the NFL.

His 3,316 yards and 25 touchdowns during his senior season would be the second-highest for a single season in school history. And now, it was time for Kirk Cousins to try his hand at the NFL.

The NFL Draft

Kirk Cousins ran into some of the same problems in the NFL draft that he did coming out of high school. His measurables just did not jump off the page at you.

"There are some who think Cousins is going to go in the second round," ESPN Draft expert Mel Kiper said. "Philadelphia Eagles reportedly had somewhat of an interest. We'll see. They have two picks in the second round. Denver, there's talk about them in the second round maybe looking at quarterback, we'll see on that. But I think a Kirk Cousins, the fact he's solid in just about all areas, size-wise, arm strength wise, adequate enough mobility—and that's not a strength but adequate enough in terms of his awareness in the pocket to get out of trouble and bide some time.

"I thought he made some bad decisions. The red zone wasn't his friend in terms some of the things that went on there—49.2% was his completion percentage in the red zone. Even against ranked teams, he had five interceptions, less than 60% there. But he's a great kid, great leader, loves the game, passionate worker, studies hard."[xxix]

Cousins was invited to the Senior Bowl but was the third-string quarterback on the North team behind Wisconsin's Russell Wilson and Kellen Moore. But Cousins used that week of practice in front of NFL coaches to help his chances.

One of the coaches there had a familiar face. Mike Singletary was an assistant coach with the Vikings and was now coaching at the Senior Bowl.

"That was cool to be coached by him in elementary school and then come full circle and I'm on the same team he's coaching at the Senior Bowl," Cousins said. "That was a moment when you say, 'Look at how far we've come.'"[xxx]

The Minnesota Vikings coaching staff was coaching the North squad, but the Washington staff was coaching the South squad. Although he was not being coached by the Washington staff, Cousins sat down for an informal 45-minute conversation with Washington Head Coach Mike Shanahan, his son and offensive coordinator Kyle Shanahan, and quarterbacks Coach Matt LaFleur.

This gave the Washington staff a chance to get to know more about Cousins and his approach to the game. It would prove to be one of the more helpful conversations that Cousins would have all week long.

"Coach Shanahan later told me after the fact that he noticed some throws that I made during that game caught his attention," Cousins said. "I think it caused him to keep an eye on me as he went back to D.C. and watched some film on the potential quarterbacks to draft. In that sense, I think it did have an impact on ending up here."[xxxi]

When the game came around, Cousins performed well. He was 5-11 for 115 yards, a touchdown, and an interception. His North squad ended up winning the game. But the game was not as important as performing well during the week leading up to the game.

"As time has passed, I think the guys who showed a lot of good things on the practice field that week and showed some playmaking ability on game day have gone on to good careers thus far," Cousins said. "I think some of the guys who were highly touted but were awfully quiet during the game and awfully quiet during the week, I haven't heard a lot from them. So, I think it was a very telling week."[xxxii]

The 2012 NFL Draft was deep with quarterbacks. Andrew Luck of Stanford was the clear favorite to be the top pick, followed by Heisman Trophy winner Robert Griffin III out of Baylor. Indianapolis held the first pick and Washington the second. That seemed to eliminate Washington as a potential suitor for Cousins after they selected Griffin as the second-overall pick.

Ryan Tannehill out of Texas A&M was selected eighth overall by Miami, and Brandon Weeden was selected 22nd by Cleveland. One quarterback was selected in the second round. By the third round, Cousins was sure that he was going to be selected.

Seattle took Cousins' college rival from Wisconsin, Russell Wilson, with the 75th pick, and Philadelphia selected Cousins' former college teammate Nick Foles, who had transferred to Arizona after his freshman year at Michigan State. Three rounds, seven quarterbacks selected, and still Cousins had not heard his name called.

Finally, in the fourth round, with the 102nd pick in the draft, Washington selected Kirk Cousins out of Michigan State. However, it seemed that Washington had already selected its franchise quarterback with the second-overall pick. It appeared that Cousins was going to be a backup again.

Chapter 3: Pro Career

Backup Again

After three years as a starter and captain at Michigan State, Kirk Cousins was a backup again in the NFL. But despite taking a quarterback with the second pick in the draft, there was controversy in the Washington camp after they selected Cousins in the fourth round.

Some in the organization viewed Cousins as the eventual starter and did not think that Griffin was worth the second pick. This caused friction between Cousins and Griffin. Griffin felt that he constantly needed to be looking over his shoulder and that Cousins was after his job.

"From the moment Kirk was drafted, I think Robert had animosity towards him. A lot of people in this area hated that fourth-round pick; I don't think anyone hated it as much as RGIII hated it," former Washington tight end Chris Cooley said. "I think it became really contentious over the last two years, to where Rex Grossman, a guy who I'm close with, said, 'This is weird in here. This is a bad situation in here. These guys don't like each other.'"[xxxiii]

Despite the animosity in the quarterback room, Cousins was the clear backup to start the season. Washington started the season 2-2 and was hosting 4-0 Atlanta in Week 5.

In the third quarter, Griffin scrambled and slid down but was hit in the head on his way down. He suffered a concussion and had to leave the game. Cousins was now set to make his professional debut.

When Griffin left the game, Washington was winning 10-7, but Atlanta quickly came down the field to take a 14-10 lead. Early in the fourth quarter, Cousins led his first scoring drive, hitting Santana Moss on a 77-yard touchdown reception.

Atlanta then scored on its next two drives to take a 24-17 lead with less than three minutes remaining. Cousins would get the ball back twice in the final two minutes of the game but threw two straight interceptions to seal the Atlanta victory.

After Washington evened their record at 3-3, the Redskins lost three straight games. Cousins did not play in any of the games. Washington did finally right itself, however, and started a three-game winning streak.

In Week 13 against Baltimore, Griffin hurt himself again. He sprained the LCL in his right knee and was forced to miss the following week. Cousins would get his first career start against Cleveland. Cousins played well as Washington blew out the Browns 38-21. But the following week, it was back to the bench.

Washington ended the season with a 10-6 record, good enough to win the NFC East. They would host Seattle in the Wild Card Round of the NFL Playoffs.

In the second quarter, Washington was clinging to a 14-13 lead when Griffin re-injured his right knee. He came out for a series but was back in the next time Washington had the ball.

Seattle, led by another rookie quarterback, Russell Wilson, took a 24-14 lead in the fourth quarter when Griffin got hurt again. This time, he stayed down on the ground, unable to walk off the field under his own power.

Cousins came in the game late but only completed 3 of 10 passes, and Washington lost the game. After the game, an MRI revealed that Griffin had torn his ACL, LCL, and meniscus on his right knee. He had surgery to repair the knee three days later.

At the start of training camp, Griffin was cleared to begin practicing but was held out for precautionary reasons. Cousins took all the snaps for the first time, with the understanding that when the time came, Griffin would take over again.

"Everyone knows—including myself—that this is Robert's team," Cousins said. "And it's my job that any time Robert's not able to play, that there's not a drop off, offensively, from Robert to myself. That's a lot to ask of myself, but that's the expectation, and I need to make sure that happens. It's my job to be a very good insurance policy."[xxxiv]

Washington started the season 2-4, and Cousins did not see the field. Cousins finally got into a Week 7 blowout loss to the Broncos but threw two interceptions.

Finally, in Week 14, Washington had a dismal 3-10 record and Coach Mike Shanahan decided to bench Griffin and start Cousins.

Cousins was able to throw three touchdowns in the game, but he also had three turnovers. Despite all that, Washington had a chance to win the game in the final minute. Cousins connected with Moss on a three-yard touchdown reception, putting Washington down by one.

Instead of kicking the extra point for the tie, Shanahan decided to go for two and the win. Cousins' pass was deflected at the line of scrimmage and fell incomplete. Atlanta won the game by a point.

"I loved the call to go for 2 there," Cousins said. "I felt like we had them on the ropes. We just didn't do enough to execute, but it starts right here with me."[xxxv]

Cousins started the final two games of the season but did not fare much better. He threw three interceptions and was sacked three times in two losses.

Washington finished the season 3-13, and Shanahan was fired at the end of the year. Jay Gruden was hired to replace Shanahan. Gruden had been the offensive coordinator for the Cincinnati Bengals.

Despite Cousins finishing the season as the starter, when the 2014 season started, Griffin was back to being the starter and Cousins was on the bench again.

After not playing in Week 1, Cousins was called on again to take over for Griffin. In the first quarter of a game against Jacksonville, Griffin dislocated his ankle and would be forced to miss the next six weeks.

Cousins took over and led Washington to a 41-10 victory over the Jaguars.

"Kirk is a true pro," Gruden said after the game. "He's handled being a backup like a pro, and now his time is going to come to really take this thing and run with it."[xxxvi]

The following week, Cousins threw for 427 yards and 2 touchdowns in a loss to the Eagles. It was the fourth-highest passing game in Washington's history.

"As an offense, as a quarterback, you just have so many people around you who can make you successful," Cousins said. "And that's what I think I take away from today is the good thing we have right now, and we obviously need to get better. But there's a lot there to work with."[xxxvii]

Despite that, there were two Cousins throws that ended up costing Washington the game. He threw an interception late in the fourth quarter and missed a wide-open receiver on a fourth-and-one with less than a minute remaining in the three-point loss.

"I think accuracy goes back to your feet," he said. "You have to always be balanced. You have to always be consistent and then you can always be accurate. When that balance and that consistency starts to change then that's where the accuracy starts to waiver and that's where I have to go back and study my footwork and make sure that I'm keeping myself balanced."[xxxviii]

But that would be the highlight of Cousins' season. Washington went on to lose four straight games, including a 45-14 loss to the New York Giants in which Cousins threw four interceptions.

After a Week 7 win over the Titans, Griffin returned to the lineup and Cousins was back on the bench. Gruden then made the decision to make Cousins the third-string quarterback behind Griffin and Colt McCoy. He was inactive for seven straight weeks, all Washington losses.

With no game plan to memorize or team to prepare for, Cousins went to work on himself and his ability as a quarterback. Cousins made the decision to go to the Neurocore Brain Performance Center. Essentially, he was trying to learn to prepare his mind for a game in the same way that you would prepare your body.

"It's kind of an abstract thing, but I call it brain performance," Cousins said. "I see it as the next frontier because you look at weightlifting in the 1950s and '60s, not every football player was lifting weights; they weren't sure about the benefit it would give you. Now everybody has a strength coach; everybody lifts weights. And I see brain training kind of being that next thing. I just want to maximize what I've got."[xxxix]

Cousins spent the remainder of the 2014 season working on himself, while Washington continued to stumble. Washington finished the season 4-12. But after the year, Cousins knew that he would have a shot at the starting quarterback position in 2015.

The Starter

In the offseason, something outside of Kirk Cousins' control happened that would change his fortunes in Washington. The team hired a new general manager. After a 4-12 season, Washington brought in Scot McCloughan as the new general manager to rebuild the team.

With no connection to any of the quarterbacks on the roster, Gruden and McCloughan opened a competition for the job. In the second preseason game, Griffin was running for his life against the Lions and suffered a concussion. He would miss the final two preseason games, giving Cousins an edge.

Just before the opening game of the season, Gruden came out and said that Washington was now "Kirk's team." For the first time in his career, Cousins would be the starter.

"There's something powerful about feeling believed in, and something powerful about knowing where you stand," Cousins said. "I can't say enough about the class act Robert has been from the day I was drafted to now. The way he has treated me, the way he has handled a lot of adversity—I have marveled at his ability as a rookie to never flinch, to compete as a young player in this league and win Rookie of the Year and taking our team to the playoffs and winning the division. I marveled at that. The way that he is a fierce competitor, I've always respected. He has always been a guy who remains classy, works very, very hard, and I've learned from that example."[xl]

Cousins' time as a starter did not begin well. Washington was 2-4 to start the season. In those six games, Cousins threw eight interceptions and only six touchdowns. But then came a pivotal Week 7 game against Tampa Bay.

For most of the first half, it appeared as though this was just going to be another Washington blowout loss. Washington found themselves down 24-0 with just over five minutes remaining in the quarter. Cousins was able to run it in for an eight-yard touchdown to cut Tampa's lead, but going into the half, Washington was still down 24-7 and looked lifeless.

Nevertheless, Washington dominated the third quarter. Cousins threw two touchdown passes and cut Tampa's lead to 24-21. Then, in the fourth quarter, Tampa managed to put up two field goals to extend the lead to 30-24. Washington got the ball back with 2:24 remaining in the game. Cousins methodically took the ball down the field and hit Jordan Reed for a game-winning six-yard touchdown pass with 24 seconds left.

While coming back from 24 points down was exciting, what happened after the game would come to define Cousins for the remainder of his career. As he was walking into the tunnel to go to the locker room, Cousins saw a local sports crew standing near the entrance to the tunnel.

Cousins had done dozens of interviews with the reporter and knew him and his crew. The camera was rolling as the players walked off the field. Cousins had just led the biggest comeback in Washington history. He looked directly into the camera and yelled, "You like that?"

The phrase would be repeated over and over and became a rallying cry for the 2015 Redskins. It would show up on shirts with Cousins selling them himself to help raise money for the International Justice Mission. But from such a low-key guy, where did this excited outburst come from?

"I don't know where it came from," Cousins said. "If I did hear it from someone else, I wouldn't be able to remember enough to cite them. It honestly just came out of having a chip on your shoulder, trying to prove yourself and having a lot of passion. I think it's been a good rallying cry for our team. Looking back at a great accomplishment, just saying, 'You like that.' It's a stamp of approval on a good performance, kinda two thumbs up."[xli]

It was not just that Washington would have a slogan for the remainder of its season, but that the Redskins had truly found their quarterback of the future in Cousins. Former first-round pick, Robert Griffin III, would remain inactive for the entire 2015 season and be released by Washington before the 2016 season.

Despite the momentum and energy that came to Washington from the come-from-behind victory, the Redskins still played inconsistently for most of the season. Heading into the final four weeks, Washington was 5-7. Their only hope to make the playoffs was to win out and win a mediocre NFC East.

That's exactly what Washington did. The Redskins would win their final four games, including tough wins over Philadelphia and Dallas, to secure the NFC East title. In those four games, Cousins threw 12 touchdowns and only one interception. He also threw for more than 300 yards in three of the four games.

Washington won the NFC East and secured a home playoff game against Aaron Rodgers and the Green Bay Packers. In his first full season as a starter, Cousins threw for 4,166 yards and 29 touchdowns. He also led the entire NFL in completion percentage at 69.8%.[xlii]

The Redskins were on fire to start the game. After a safety and a field goal, Cousins connected with Reed on a 24-yard touchdown to give Washington an 11-0 lead. But after that, it was all Green Bay. The Packers scored the next 17 points to take a 17-11 lead into the half. Cousins got the lead back for Washington in the second half, scoring on a three-yard run. But again, Green Bay was too much. The Packers scored the game's final 18 points to win 35-18.

Despite outplaying Rodgers in the game, Cousins was headed home. It was his first career playoff start, and it ended in disappointment. It would not be the last time for Cousins.

After the 2015 season, Kirk Cousins was set to become a free agent. Instead, Washington signed him to a non-exclusive franchise tender. The deal guaranteed Cousins $20 million for 2016, but it also allowed him to negotiate with another team. If another team chose to sign him, they would have to give Washington two first-round picks. No team offered Cousins a contract, so he signed his one-year deal with Washington.

Washington's inconsistent play continued into 2016. After two straight losses to start the season, despite Cousins throwing for more than 300 yards in both games, Washington went on to win four straight games.

In Week 8, Washington traveled to London to take on the Bengals. The Redskins tied the score with 40 seconds remaining in the game. Neither one of the teams would put up any points in overtime and Washington settled for the tie. At the time, it would not seem to be a big deal, but it would be that tie that would come to haunt Washington's season.

On the last day of the season, Washington took on the Giants with a simple playoff equation: win and they were in. The Detroit Lions were already 9-7 and Washington was 8-6-1 heading into the game. All Washington had to do was beat the Giants, who had already clinched a playoff spot and had nothing to play for.

Washington's offense did nothing for the first three-quarters of the game, managing only a field goal. Finally, Cousins hit Jordan Reed on a one-yard touchdown pass to tie the game at 10. But that would be the last gasp for the Redskins.

New York took a three-point lead with a little over two minutes remaining. On the ensuing possession, Cousins threw his second interception of the quarter. Washington got the ball back deep in its own territory, but New York recovered a fumbled flea-flicker and returned it for a touchdown as time expired. And to add insult to injury, the Giants went for two on the conversion.

"This isn't my first time dealing with this," said Cousins, who was sacked a season-high four times. "Tough times don't last; tough people do, right? I sound like a broken record, but I'm going to keep saying that until I retire."[xliii]

Cousins had his best season as a starter for Washington. He threw for 4,917 yards and 25 touchdowns and was named to the Pro Bowl for the first time in his career.

Heading into the offseason after another year ended with a disappointing loss, Kirk was supposed to be a free agent. Washington had signed him to the non-exclusive franchise tag prior to the 2016 season.

The two sides worked to find common ground on a long-term contract but could not come to a deal. So, with no deal in sight, the Redskins once again placed the non-exclusive franchise tag on Cousins. It was the first time in NFL history that the tag was placed on a quarterback in two consecutive seasons.

Cousins had reason to want a long-term contract from Washington. He had set the team record for passing attempts, completions, yards, and 300-yard games in 2016. He also led the team to an NFC East title in his first season as a starter.

"I want to be where I'm wanted and if they tag mean that tells you that you're wanted," Cousins said. "They are not going to tag you or commit to you if they don't want you. So, if they tag me then that's great and it means they want me back. Whether I sign a five-year deal or a one-year franchise tag, I'm going to feel like I'm on a one year deal every year and have to prove myself week in and week out. If they tag me great it looks like I'm wanted. If they don't then that sends a strong message too and let's go look at our options."[xliv]

It seemed that even Washington's Coach Jay Gruden wanted to keep his quarterback on a long-term deal, but the sides just could not get together on a number.

"He's done a lot of great things, there's no question about it," Gruden said. "Any time that you throw for almost 5,000 yards in an NFL season, there's a lot of positives there. This is his second full year playing and he's learned a lot, but he's got a lot more to learn, both from a mental side and then from a physical side, maybe the ability to create some plays once in a while would be good—like he did against Chicago. A couple scramble first downs, some off-schedule plays that you see some of these guys make. Athletically, he's not like Russell Wilson, or some of those guys, but still, maybe if he can buy time in the pocket a little bit, something he can continue to work on, get a feel for [and] take his game to the next level. He's already at a very high level."[xlv]

For the second straight season, Cousins headed into the year without a long-term contract with Washington.

Unfortunately for Cousins, he spent most of the 2017 season running for his life. He was sacked a career-high 41 times and set career highs in rushing yards and attempts. Since he was not a running quarterback, Washington did not design plays for Cousins to run. Instead, whenever the rush got close, he would take off.

In Week 7 against Seattle, Cousins was sacked six times, including once for a safety. Washington went into the game without three starters on the offensive line. Despite all that, Cousins was able to drive the Redskins 70 yards in 35 seconds to score the game-winning touchdown with less than a minute left in the game to even Washington's record at 4-4.

It would be the last highlight for Washington that season. In the final week of the season, Washington lost to the New York Giants 18-10. The two teams only managed one field goal in the second half. Cousins had a miserable game, throwing three interceptions.

After the game, the story was not about Cousins' interceptions or Washington finishing the season at 7-9—it was about Cousins' future with the team.

"We have to have stability at that position, somehow, some way. Not everybody has it," Redskins coach Jay Gruden said. "That's the way it is in pro football nowadays. If you've got one, you'd like to keep one. We'll have to make that decision here pretty soon. Kirk will also. It's not totally up to us. Kirk's got to buy in also."[xlvi]

Two and a half months later, Kirk Cousins signed the biggest guaranteed contract in NFL history at the time. He signed a three-year, $84-million contract with the Minnesota Vikings. It would make him the highest-paid player in the league, at least temporarily.

NFL contracts, unlike those in the NBA or MLB, are not guaranteed. So, if a player gets hurt, the team does not have to pay them for the following season. Cousins' contract with Minnesota was the first in the history of the NFL that would guarantee his entire salary for all three years he would be with Minnesota.

After the uncertainty of two seasons in Washington playing under the franchise tag, Cousins was now getting generational wealth for himself and his family.

"Players after me will have to decide what they want to do," Cousins said about his contract. "There is nothing I can pave unless other people come after me. We'll have to look back and see how this league goes from here. Winning is what I said it would be all about, and it's true," Cousins said. "I think it's the best chance, and that's what truly matters."[xlvii]

Now, it was off to Minnesota.

Up to the Great North

When Cousins arrived in Minnesota, expectations were high. He was coming off three straight 4,000-yard passing seasons and had helped Washington win two NFC East titles, one as a starter and the other as a backup. It was the first NFC East Championship for Washington since 1999.

Minnesota had won the NFC North title twice since 2015 but had only one playoff win to show for it since 2010. Their division was dominated by Aaron Rodgers and the Green Bay Packers. Since 2011, Green Bay has won eight division titles compared to Minnesota's two.

Cousins had a personal grudge against Rodgers as well. It was Rodgers and the Packers that had knocked him out of the playoffs in 2015, his first year as a starter with Washington and his only playoff start, up to that time.

Cousins had a great debut for the Vikings in a 24-16 win over the 49ers. He threw for 244 yards and 2 touchdowns but, more importantly, no turnovers.

"I'm so grateful for this opportunity that I've been given, and I just want to make good on it with every chance I get," said Cousins after the game.

Despite the win, Cousins was still running for his life. He was sacked three times by the 49ers' defense. In the Vikings' first four games, the team was 1-2-1. Cousins was sacked 13 times in those four games but threw only two interceptions.

The Vikings' inconsistent play continued throughout the remainder of the season, but Cousins continued to play well for Minnesota. As the season wound down, it appeared the tie was going to hurt a Kirk Cousins team once again. On the final week of the season, Minnesota was hosting Chicago with a chance to make the playoffs.

For the second time in three seasons, Cousins had a chance to get his team into the playoffs with a win. And much like two seasons ago, the Bears had already clinched the NFC North title and had nothing to play for. Two years earlier, Cousins and Washington lost to the New York Giants in the season's final game with a chance to make the playoffs with a win.

In the first half, the Minnesota offense did nothing. Finally, down 10-0 late in the second quarter, the Vikings got a drive going but had to settle for a field goal. Cousins and wide receiver Adam Thielen were seen arguing on the sideline just before the half.

Minnesota did manage a third-quarter touchdown to get within three, but Chicago scored the game's final 10 points for a 24-10 victory. The loss sent Minnesota home.

Cousins had just finished his fourth season as a starter, three in Washington and one with Minnesota. In those three seasons, he was 0-3 in win-or-go-home games, and he was 0-9 in primetime games. For better or worse, Cousins was starting to get a reputation as a quarterback who could not win a big game. In some circles, he started to receive the nickname "One O'clock Kirk" for his ability to play well in games that were played early in the day. The nickname was a slap in the face as it pointed out Cousins' inability to close the deal in the big games.

With this burden hanging around his neck, Cousins entered the 2019 season. Minnesota alternated wins and losses for the first four games but then went on a four-game winning streak. In those games, Cousins averaged 315 yards per game and threw 10 touchdowns.

For his efforts, Cousins was named the NFC Offensive Player of the Month for October. In Week 12, the

Vikings hosted the Seahawks on *Monday Night Football*. Cousins played well, but Minnesota still lost the game 37-30. That loss extended Cousins' losing streak as a starter on Monday night to eight games. He was 0-8 in his career in *Monday Night Football* games.

The season ended with Minnesota at 10-6, good enough to clinch the final wild-card spot. Cousins ended the year with 3,603 yards and 26 touchdowns. It was the least number of yards he threw for in his five seasons as a starter, but he only threw six interceptions, which was also a career low. It was also the first time in his career that he led a team to 10 wins. For his efforts, Cousins was selected to his second career Pro Bowl.

Minnesota had to play its Wild Card game at the New Orleans Superdome against the Saints and future Hall-of-Fame quarterback Drew Brees. On an average Sunday, it was a difficult place to play, but this was the Playoffs, making it virtually impossible.

The two teams traded points in the first half, with Minnesota taking a 13-10 lead into the half. In the third quarter, Minnesota dominated the action but only came away with a Dalvin Cook touchdown for a 20-10 lead.

Brees was just getting warmed up. He threw a touchdown pass early in the fourth quarter and then drove the Saints 39 yards in seven plays to kick the game-tying field goal with less than five seconds remaining.

On the first possession of overtime, Cousins and the Vikings drove the ball down the field, going 75 yards. Cousins hit tight end Kyle Rudolph on a fade for the game-winning touchdown.

The Superdome went silent, and the Minnesota players mobbed Cousins and Rudolph.

"I'm just glad Kirk can't win big games, apparently," Rudolph said. "We proved that one wrong today."[xlviii]

Cousins had a brilliant game, throwing for 242 yards and the game's biggest touchdown. It was his first career playoff win.

"I'm just happy we won," Cousins said. "It was a great, great game, two good football teams. Being a fourth-round pick and kind of working your way up in the league—now you win a playoff game. Guess what? You look around and you realize there's more mountains to climb. You just keep chasing the next mountain and there will always be people who are going to criticize you—and that's OK."[xlix]

The win earned Minnesota a trip to San Francisco. The 49ers were the top overall seed in the NFC and were known for their dominating defense.

And that formidable defense came to play against the Vikings. Cousins was able to keep the game close in the first half, but Minnesota never got close to a score in the second half. Cousins was sacked a season-high six times and threw an interception in the second half that led to a touchdown. In the end, San Francisco walked away with a dominating 27-10 win, sending the Vikings home for the season.

"We didn't do enough offensively to give ourselves a chance to win the game," Cousins said. "It hurts right now. It's so raw right now, just falling short."[1]

COVID-19

The 2020 season was upended, as was everything else in life, by the COVID-19 epidemic. The NFL had an advantage over the MLB and NBA, however, both of whom were in the middle of their seasons when the virus hit America. The NFL was in the offseason and had months to study how to safely and effectively bring its players back into the locker room and team facilities and eventually back onto the playing field.

But for a while, Kirk Cousins refused to follow the NFL's safety protocols.

"I want to respect what other people's concerns are," Cousins said. "For me personally, just talking no one else can get the virus, what is your concern if you could get it, I would say I'm gonna go about my daily life. If I get it, I'm gonna ride it out. I'm gonna let nature do its course. Survival-of-the-fittest kind of approach. And just say, if it knocks me out, it knocks me out. I'm going to be OK. You know, even if I die. If I die, I die. I kind of have peace about that."[li]

Cousins would later walk those comments back and said that he planned on abiding by the NFL's rules.

Perhaps the drama surrounding Cousins and his views on COVID-19 caused some friction in the locker room as the Vikings got off to a 1-5 start. In those six games, Cousins was picked off 10 times and sacked 14 times. He threw 10 touchdowns as well. The 10 interceptions were more than what Cousins threw in the entire previous season.

The Vikings did manage to get their record to 6-6 after beating all three of their division opponents in a row. But with four games remaining, the Vikings fell short, losing three in a row.

In the season's final game, the Vikings traveled to Detroit. In one of the best games of his career, Cousins threw for a career-high 405 yards and 3 touchdowns in a two-point victory.

After the game, Cousins commented that the Vikings were close to the playoffs but missed out by two games.

In the 2021 offseason, Cousins' issues with COVID-19 popped back up again—this time in the form of his refusal to get vaccinated against the virus. Early in the preseason, Cousins was put on the Vikings' COVID-19 list after coming into contact with another quarterback who tested positive. It was only after he was placed on the COVID-19 list that it was revealed that Cousins was not vaccinated.

"So, I'm going to be vigilant about avoiding a close contact," Cousins said. "I've even thought about, should I even set up, literally, Plexiglas around where I sit, so that this could never happen again? I thought about it, 'cause I'm gonna do whatever it takes."[lii]

Shortly after it was revealed that Cousins was not vaccinated, his father gave a speech critical of COVID-19 vaccines and vaccine policies. After that, Holland Hospital in Holland, Michigan, cut ties with Cousins. He had been the hospital's spokesman.

"While we acknowledge that each person is entitled to their own viewpoints, those who speak on our behalf must support messages that align with the hospital's position on matters of vital importance to individual and community health. For this reason, Holland Hospital will discontinue using Kirk Cousins as our spokesperson for now. We are proud of our association with Kirk. He embodies many values we respect and share as part of our work culture. However, we must be certain that our communications about COVID-19 vaccination are consistent and unequivocal," the hospital said in a statement.[liii]

The controversy once again hurt the Vikings to start the season. Minnesota started out the year 1-3. The Vikings were 4-5 when they hosted Green Bay in one of the most exciting games of the season.

The Vikings played their best game of the year, and Rodgers and Cousins had a shootout for the ages. Minnesota opened a 16-3 lead after Cousins hit Adam Thielen, but Rodgers came back with a touchdown just before the half.

Cousins then opened the second half with a touchdown pass to Justin Jefferson, giving Minnesota a 23-10 lead. Nonetheless, Rodgers came right back with two straight touchdowns to put Green Bay up by one.

With 2:17 left in the game, Cousins threw his third touchdown of the game to put Minnesota up by seven.

But on the very next play, Rodgers connected on a 75-yard touchdown pass.

With just over two minutes remaining in the exciting slugfest, Cousins went 5-5 on the final drive, getting the ball deep in Green Bay territory. And just as time expired, Minnesota hit the game-winning field goal.

"It's just life in the NFL. It's exciting. I certainly understand why people want to follow and watch it," Cousins said.[liv]

Beating Green Bay in such a thrilling game could have been something that turned Minnesota's season around, but the Vikings dropped their next two games, essentially ending their season.

Furthermore, two days before the rematch with Green Bay, Cousins tested positive for COVID-19 and was forced to miss the game. Minnesota subsequently lost the game by 17 points to the Packers in the rematch.

Minnesota finished the season at 8-8, just missing out on the playoffs. Cousins threw for 4,221 yards and was named to the Pro Bowl for the third time in his career.

With COVID-19 behind him, Cousins was looking to take the Vikings to the next level. Cousins was entering his eighth season as a starter but he still only had one playoff win.

The 2022 season started out with a crushing win over the Packers. Cousins threw for 277 yards and 2 touchdowns. He followed that up with his worst game of the season against the Eagles. Cousins threw three interceptions against the eventual NFC Champions in a 24-7 defeat.

The season was starting to look like another lost Vikings year, but that was when things started to come together. Minnesota won their next seven games in a row to improve to 8-1 on the season.

The winning streak came to an end in inexplicable fashion with a 40-3 loss to the Cowboys. It was

Minnesota's worst home loss in 59 years. Cousins was sacked eight times in the game, including a strip sack by Micah Parsons.

"I just think there you need to have two hands on the football," said Cousins. "When you watch it and coach it and look at how to improve, if you're holding on with two hands as you're running, it's less likely to be a fumble there."[lv]

For Cousins, the dismal game snapped his streak of 39 straight with at least one touchdown pass. It also brought back the rumblings that he could not win the big game.

"At this point in the season, November comes and sometimes you can get hit in the mouth. This league has a way of humbling any team, at any point in time, if you do not play good football," Vikings coach Kevin O'Connell said after the game.[lvi]

The Vikings were able to bounce back easily, however, winning four of their next five games. Minnesota was sitting at 12-3 with a chance for a first-round bye in the playoffs if they could win out. But standing between them and a bye were the Green Bay Packers.

Cousins threw three interceptions in the game, and Green Bay blew out the Vikings 41-17.

"I just didn't play well enough tonight," Cousins said. "Just need to play better, that's the bottom line."[lvii]

Minnesota ended the season over the hapless Bears to finish the year at 13-4. It was the best record that Cousins ever had in his NFL career. He threw for a career-high 4,547 yards and 29 touchdowns. He was named to the Pro Bowl for the fourth time in his career.

The Vikings opened the playoffs by hosting the New York Giants. Cousins started the scoring with a one-yard touchdown run. The Giants immediately responded with two scores to take a 14-7 lead after the first quarter. Then, after a New York field goal, Cousins led the Vikings down the field for another touchdown to cut the lead to three just before the half.

The Giants took the opening kickoff of the second half right down the field for another touchdown, but Cousins immediately responded with a touchdown pass of his own.

The Vikings tied the score in the fourth quarter, but Saquon Barkley scored a Giants' touchdown with seven minutes remaining. The teams exchanged punts, and the Vikings got the ball with two minutes remaining.

Cousins was able to get the ball into Giants territory, but on third down, he completed a short pass, setting up a fourth and eight. Cousins dropped back to pass and hit tight end T.J. Hockenson on a three-yard crossing route. He was immediately tackled by several Giants defenders, ending the game.

"There was always belief. I think that's why it hurts, because you expect to find a way, especially the way this team has gone all year," said Cousins after the game.[lviii]

After the game, Cousins also said that this was the toughest loss of his career. The whispers started to get louder that Cousins could not win the big game. Cousins also got questions about why he threw the ball three yards on the final play of the game when the Vikings needed eight.

"I had thrown short of the sticks on a few different occasions in the game, and even going back a few weeks, and just felt like throwing short of the sticks isn't the end of the world," Cousins said. "It was obviously tight coverage so he didn't have a chance to pull away. I thought I was going to go down and take a sack if I didn't put it up."[lix]

O'Connell took some of the blame for the play call in that moment.

"The intent as a play caller is you're not going to call a primary concept where somebody's short of the sticks, especially if it's fourth down," O'Connell said. "Looking back on it, maybe I could have been a little bit more, 'Hey, this is where you want the ball to go.' But I want Kirk to be able to play and be free out there to make good decisions. He did all night long. In the end, I look at it as it's as much on me with that play call, even though we had [eligible receivers] with a chance [to get] down the field maybe. There's always a play that could be better."[lx]

Despite both Cousins and O'Connell taking the blame for the loss, Vikings fans were not having it. *The Sporting News* even went so far as to refer to Cousins as a "Costco Hot Dog," meaning that he looks good, but you always regret choosing it.

Cousins will turn 35 just before the start of the 2023 season and is heading into the final year of his deal with the Vikings. He recently restructured his contract to help Minnesota get under the cap for the 2023 season. He is still looking for an extension that will keep him in Minnesota for the rest of his career.

"I think everybody's gotta do their due diligence," Cousins said. "I'm looking forward to this year and wanting to go out there and prove it again, do it again and play at the highest level I can. That's really where my focus is. Nobody can operate with entitlement or comfort and put in less than their best. Teams can do whatever they want to do. That's their prerogative. You just go to work, do the best you can. I'm encouraged and excited because I do think I have a lot of good football ahead of me. Gotta go out there and earn that, but I feel positive about the future looking forward."[lxi]

It remains to be seen if Cousins will remain in Minnesota or head for greener pastures.

Chapter 4: Personal Life

In 2012, Kirk Cousins met Julie Hampton through a mutual friend. She was a teacher who was living in Georgia while he was a football player in Washington.

A few months into dating, Kirk purchased a book called *101 Questions to Ask Before You Get Engaged*. He later said that they got through most of them. About 18 months later, Kirk popped the question in a most unusual way.

"I talked to my U.S. congressman from my home area in West Michigan, Bill Huizenga, who I had gotten to know a little bit," Kirk said. "I called him to see if I could propose on the balcony of the Speaker of the House's office, because I had been there before and seen the view and thought it was a great view. He said they could set it up."[lxii]

The view from the Speaker of the House's office looks directly down the National Mall to the Washington Monument and the Lincoln Memorial just beyond that.

The only issue would be finding a date. They had to find a time when Cousins had a home game, and the Speaker of the House would not be in his office.

"I was extremely nervous," Kirk said. "On the way down driving the car, as we got close to the Capital building, I was holding her hand and she goes 'Why are your hands cold and sweaty?' I said, 'I don't know,' but it was because I was super nervous."[lxiii]

Kirk was able to convince Julie to come up to the Speaker's office to see the view.

"I just mentioned the view and told her how we'd gotten to know each other in this city and how we had good memories when we used to walk through the city on some of our earlier dates," Kirk said. "I went down on a knee before it got too sappy, before it got too awkward. I don't remember exactly what she said, but she said 'yes.' That's all I needed to hear."[lxiv]

Kirk and Julie were married on June 28, 2014, in Atlanta, Georgia. The couple has two boys, Cooper and Turner. During the summers, the Cousins family returns to Michigan, where Kirk grew up. They have a house on a lake and recently purchased the Clear Brook Golf Course in Saugatuck, Michigan.

In 2019, the Cousins formed the Julie and Kirk Cousins Foundation. The goal of the foundation is to "Transform Worldly Resources into Heavenly Riches through Extravagant Generosity."

Through the Foundation, Kirk and Julie have donated thousands of dollars to worthy causes around the globe, including the Boys and Girls Club, International Justice Mission, and Kirk's high school, Holland Christian School.

After Kirk found his motto with, "You like that," he transformed the slogan into a t-shirt and sold it to benefit the Julie and Kirk Cousins Foundation.

In 2021, Kirk made a $500,000 donation to the Minnesota Vikings Social Justice Committee.

"For me, or really for my wife and I, and our family foundation, it was really a no-brainer," Cousins said about the donation. "We've observed the work that our social justice group here with the Vikings and our locker room has done, really, since before I got here. It's just been very impressive the way players have led, and there's been players very involved. And I've observed and just been really impressed. So, we wanted to get involved in the community, and we thought it's a no-brainer to just go through right where I go to work every day, the people we know, and it just made a lot of sense."[lxv]

Kirk Cousins has made a difference in thousands of lives around the globe through his charity work and will continue to do so for the remainder of his life.

Chapter 5: Legacy

Fairly or unfairly, quarterbacks are judged on one statistic: wins. And more importantly and specifically—Super Bowl and playoff wins. That may be the knock on Cousins' legacy. Despite having the better team at times, including in the 2022 Playoffs against the Giants, Cousins only has one playoff win in his career.

Throughout his career, Cousins has not just come up short in the playoffs but also in big regular season games. His teams lost win-or-go-home games twice in three seasons. For most of his career, he had not won a single prime-time game.

This lack of big game wins also dogged Peyton Manning throughout his career, but Manning was able to put all that to rest by winning the Super Bowl. At 35, to start the 2023 season, a Super Bowl win seems to be a long way away from Cousins.

With only eight seasons as a starter, Cousins has terrific numbers. He currently ranks 28th in NFL history with 37,140 passing yards, and 23rd in passing touchdowns with 252. By the time his career ends, he will easily be in the top 20 in both categories, and possibly even the top 15.

But do his statistics make him an automatic Hall of Famer? Probably not. He has never been in the top 10 in MVP voting and has never been first team All-Pro, meaning that he was never considered the best quarterback in the league.

With at least another four or five years in the NFL, Kirk still has time to prove his critics wrong and further define his legacy. But even if his career were to end today, he was still able to achieve more than anyone could have believed when he was selected in the fourth round out of Michigan State. Cousins has risen from humble unknown backup to one of the league's most accomplished and respected starting quarterbacks—that's not bad for a kid who did not get his first scholarship offer until halfway through his senior year of high school! In terms of his legacy, Cousins' success in the NFL shows that dedication, diligence, and determination can take you a very long way. Where he goes from here, we'll just have to see.

Final Word/About the Author

I was born and raised in Norwalk, Connecticut. Growing up, I could often be found spending many nights watching basketball, soccer, and football matches with my father in the family living room. I love sports and everything that sports can embody. I believe that sports are one of the most genuine forms of competition, heart, and determination. I write my works to learn more about influential athletes in the hopes that from my writing, you the reader can walk away inspired to put in an equal if not greater amount of hard work and perseverance to pursue your goals. If you enjoyed *Kirk Cousins: The Inspiring Story of One of Football's Star Quarterbacks,* please leave a review! Also, you can read more of my works on *David Ortiz, Cody Bellinger, Alex Bregman, Francisco Lindor, Shohei Ohtani, Ronald Acuna Jr., Javier Baez, Jose Altuve, Christian Yelich, Max Scherzer, Mookie Betts, Pete Alonso, Clayton Kershaw, Mike Trout, Bryce Harper, Jackie Robinson, Justin Verlander, Derek*

Jeter, Ichiro Suzuki, Ken Griffey Jr., Babe Ruth, Aaron Judge, Novak Djokovic, Roger Federer, Rafael Nadal, Serena Williams, Naomi Osaka, Coco Gauff, Baker Mayfield, George Kittle, Matt Ryan, Matthew Stafford, Eli Manning, Khalil Mack, Davante Adams, Terry Bradshaw, Jimmy Garoppolo, Philip Rivers, Von Miller, Aaron Donald, Joey Bosa, Josh Allen, Mike Evans, Joe Burrow, Carson Wentz Adam Thielen, Stefon Diggs, Lamar Jackson, Dak Prescott, Patrick Mahomes, Odell Beckham Jr., J.J. Watt, Colin Kaepernick, Aaron Rodgers, Tom Brady, Russell Wilson, Peyton Manning, Drew Brees, Calvin Johnson, Brett Favre, Rob Gronkowski, Andrew Luck, Richard Sherman, Bill Belichick, Candace Parker, Skylar Diggins-Smith, A'ja Wilson, Lisa Leslie, Sue Bird, Diana Taurasi, Julius Erving, Clyde Drexler, John Havlicek, Oscar Robertson, Ja Morant, Gary Payton, Khris Middleton, Michael Porter Jr., Julius Randle, Jrue Holiday, Domantas Sabonis, Mike Conley Jr., Jerry West, Dikembe Mutombo, Fred

VanVleet, Jamal Murray, Zion Williamson, Brandon Ingram, Jaylen Brown, Charles Barkley, Trae Young, Andre Drummond, JJ Redick, DeMarcus Cousins, Wilt Chamberlain, Bradley Beal, Rudy Gobert, Aaron Gordon, Kristaps Porzingis, Nikola Vucevic, Andre Iguodala, Devin Booker, John Stockton, Jeremy Lin, Chris Paul, Pascal Siakam, Jayson Tatum, Gordon Hayward, Nikola Jokic, Bill Russell, Victor Oladipo, Luka Doncic, Ben Simmons, Shaquille O'Neal, Joel Embiid, Donovan Mitchell, Damian Lillard, Giannis Antetokounmpo, Chris Bosh, Kemba Walker, Isaiah Thomas, DeMar DeRozan, Amar'e Stoudemire, Al Horford, Yao Ming, Marc Gasol, Draymond Green, Kawhi Leonard, Dwyane Wade, Ray Allen, Pau Gasol, Dirk Nowitzki, Jimmy Butler, Paul Pierce, Manu Ginobili, Pete Maravich, Larry Bird, Kyle Lowry, Jason Kidd, David Robinson, LaMarcus Aldridge, Derrick Rose, Paul George, Kevin Garnett, Michael Jordan, LeBron James, Kyrie Irving, Klay Thompson, Stephen Curry, Kevin Durant, Russell Westbrook,

Chris Paul, Blake Griffin, Kobe Bryant, Anthony Davis, Joakim Noah, Scottie Pippen, Carmelo Anthony, Kevin Love, Grant Hill, Tracy McGrady, Vince Carter, Patrick Ewing, Karl Malone, Tony Parker, Allen Iverson, Hakeem Olajuwon, Reggie Miller, Michael Carter-Williams, James Harden, John Wall, Tim Duncan, Steve Nash, Gregg Popovich, Pat Riley, John Wooden, Steve Kerr, Brad Stevens, Red Auerbach, Doc Rivers, Erik Spoelstra, Mike D'Antoni, and *Phil Jackson* in the Kindle Store. If you love football, check out my website at claytongeoffreys.com to join my exclusive list where I let you know about my latest books and give you lots of goodies.

Like what you read? Please leave a review!

I write because I love sharing the stories of influential athletes like Kirk Cousins with fantastic readers like you. My readers inspire me to write more so please do not hesitate to let me know what you thought by leaving a review! If you love books on life, sports, or productivity, check out my website at claytongeoffreys.com to join my exclusive list where I let you know about my latest books. Aside from being the first to hear about my latest releases, you can also download a free copy of *33 Life Lessons: Success Principles, Career Advice & Habits of Successful People*. See you there!

Clayton

References

[i] McCormick, Brittany. "Kirk Cousins: Leading his Way into History." MSU Spartans.Com. Oct. 17, 2011. Web.

[ii] Babbit, Alan. "MSU QB Kirk Cousins has a Big Supporter in Big Brother." The Holland Sentinel. Dec. 24, 2010.

[iii] Babbit, Alan. "MSU QB Kirk Cousins has a Big Supporter in Big Brother." The Holland Sentinel. Dec. 24, 2010.

[iv] Babbit, Alan. "MSU QB Kirk Cousins has a Big Supporter in Big Brother." The Holland Sentinel. Dec. 24, 2010.

[v] Tomasson, Chris. "Vikings' Kirk Cousins Learned Early About Football from Bears Great Mike Singletary." Pioneer Press. Nov. 16, 2018.

[vi] Tomasson, Chris. "Vikings' Kirk Cousins Learned Early About Football from Bears Great Mike Singletary." Pioneer Press. Nov. 16, 2018.

[vii] Yotter, Tim. "Former Bears Fan Kirk Cousins has Fond Childhood Memories." 247Sports.Com. Nov. 13, 2018. Web.

[viii] Skipper, Clay. "Kirk Cousins Believes. But Does Anyone Else?" GQ Magazine. August 28, 2017.

[ix] Skipper, Clay. "Kirk Cousins Believes. But Does Anyone Else?" GQ Magazine. August 28, 2017.

[x] Staples, Andy. "Spartans' Cousins has Beaten Odds to Become Face of Big Ten." Sports Illustrated. Oct. 21, 2011.

[xi] Staples, Andy. "Spartans' Cousins has Beaten Odds to Become Face of Big Ten." Sports Illustrated. Oct. 21, 2011.

[xii] Skipper, Clay. "Kirk Cousins Believes. But Does Anyone Else?" GQ Magazine. August 28, 2017.

[xiii] Staples, Andy. "Spartans' Cousins has Beaten Odds to Become Face of Big Ten." Sports Illustrated. Oct. 21, 2011.

[xiv] Staples, Andy. "Spartans' Cousins has Beaten Odds to Become Face of Big Ten." Sports Illustrated. Oct. 21, 2011.

[xv] Staples, Andy. "Spartans' Cousins has Beaten Odds to Become Face of Big Ten." Sports Illustrated. Oct. 21, 2011.

[xvi] Staples, Andy. "Spartans' Cousins has Beaten Odds to Become Face of Big Ten." Sports Illustrated. Oct. 21, 2011.

[xvii] McCormick, Brittany. "Kirk Cousins: Leading His Way Into History." MSU Spartans.Com. Oct. 17, 2011. Web.

[xviii] "Pryor, Ohio State Build a Quick Lead in Victory over Michigan State." ESPN.Com. Oct. 19, 2008. Web.

[xix] McCormick, Brittany. "Kirk Cousins: Leading the Way Into History." MSU Spartans.Com. Oct. 17, 2011. Web.

[xx] McCormick, Brittany. "Kirk Cousins: Leading the Way Into History." MSU Spartans.Com. Oct. 17, 2011. Web.
[xxi] McCormick, Brittany. "Kirk Cousins: Leading the Way Into History." MSU Spartans.Com. Oct. 17, 2011. Web
[xxii] McCormick, Brittany. "Kirk Cousins: Leading the Way Into History." MSU Spartans.Com. Oct. 17, 2011. Web
[xxiii] "Ricky Stanzi, Iowa Push Michigan State From the Ranks of the Unbeaten." ESPN.Com. Oct. 30, 2010 Web.
[xxiv] Babbitt, Alan. "MSU QB Kirk Cousins has Big Supporter in Big Brother." The Holland Sentinel. Dec. 24, 2010.
[xxv] "Michigan State Shocks Wisconsin with Hail Mary From Kirk Cousins to Keith Nichol." ESPN.Com. Oct. 20, 2011. Web.
[xxvi] "Nebraska's Defense Shuts Down Michigan State." ESPN.Com. Oct. 29, 2011. Web.
[xxvii] "Montee Ball's Four Touchdowns Spark Wisconsin to Big Ten Title." ESPN.Com. Dec. 4, 2011. Web.
[xxviii] "Michigan State Rallies for Three Overtime Win at the Outback Bowl." ESPN.Com. Jan. 1, 2012. Web.
[xxix] Couch, Graham. "ESPN's Mel Kiper Concerned About Kirk Cousins Decisions in the Red Zone." Mlive.Com. April 20, 2012. Web.
[xxx] Tomasson, Chris. "Vikings Kirk Cousins Learned Early About Football from Bears Great Mike Singletary." Pioneer Press. Nove. 16, 2018.
[xxxi] "Kirk Cousins' Career Altered at Senior Bowl." Commanders.Com. Jan. 24, 2014. Web.
[xxxii] "Kirk Cousins' Career Altered at Senior Bowl." Commanders.Com. Jan. 24, 2014. Web.
[xxxiii] Hendrick, Jaclyn. "RG3 Had it Out for Kirk Cousins From the Start." The New York Post. March 9, 2016.
[xxxiv] Jones, Mike. "Kirk Cousins Doesn't See Sharing Training Camp Starting Role With Griffin as Problematic." The Washington Post. July 24, 2013.
[xxxv] "Redskins Commit Seven Turnovers in Loss to Falcons.' ESPN.Com. Dec. 16, 2013. Web.
[xxxvi] Mihoces, Gary. "Redskins Lose Robert Griffin III; Kirk Cousins Steps Up." USA Today. Sept. 14, 2014.
[xxxvii] "Cousins Dazzles in First Start of 2014." Washington Commanders.Com. Sept. 22, 2014. Web.
[xxxviii] "Cousins Dazzles in First Start of 2014." Washington Commanders.Com. Sept. 22, 2014. Web.
[xxxix] "After Discouraging 2014 Season, Kirk Cousins Sought Help for his

Head." SBS News.Com. April 15, 2014. Web.

[xl] "Kirk Cousins Named Redskins' Starting Quarterback for 2015 Season." ESPN.Com. Aug. 31, 2015. Web.

[xli] Zawacki Roy, Tory. "How Kirk Cousins 'You Like That' Became a Washington Rallying Cry." ESPN.Com. Jan. 9, 2016. Web.

[xlii] "Kirk Cousins 2015 Game Log." Pro-Football Focus.Com. 2020. Web.

[xliii] "Redskins Lose to Giants 19-10, Blow Chance at Playoffs." ESPN.Com. Jan. 1, 2017. Web.

[xliv] Kring-Schreifeis. "Washington Places Exclusive Franchise Tag on Kirk Cousins." Washington Redskins.Com. Feb. 28, 2017. Web.

[xlv] Kring-Schreifeis. "Washington Places Exclusive Franchise Tag on Kirk Cousins." Washington Redskins.Com. Feb. 28, 2017. Web.

[xlvi] "Giants Close Dismal Season with a 18-10 Win Over Washington." ESPN.Com. Dec. 31, 2017 Web.

[xlvii] "Kirk Cousins Officially Signs $84 million, three year deal with Vikings." USA Today. March 15, 2018.

[xlviii] "Cook, Vikings Upend Saints, 26-20 in OT in NFL Playoffs." ESPN.Com. Jan. 5, 2020. Web.

[xlix] "Cook, Vikings Upend Saints, 26-20 in OT in NFL Playoffs." ESPN.Com. Jan. 5, 2020. Web.

[l] "49ers Win First Playoff Game in 6 Years, 27-10 Over Vikings." ESPN.Com. Jan. 11, 2020. Web.

[li] Rivera, Joe. "Kirk Cousins' Vaccination Comments: What the Vikings Quarterback Has Said." The Sporting News. Oct. 31, 2021.

[lii] Rivera, Joe. "Kirk Cousins' Vaccination Comments: What the Vikings Quarterback Has Said." The Sporting News. Oct. 31, 2021.

[liii] Rivera, Joe. "Kirk Cousins' Vaccination Comments: What the Vikings Quarterback Has Said." The Sporting News. Oct. 31, 2021.

[liv] "Vikings Outlast Rodgers, Packers 34-31 on Game-Ending Field Goal." ESPN.Com. Nov. 21, 2021. Web.

[lv] Goessling, Ben. "Vikings Suffer Worst Home Loss in 59 Years in 40-3 Smackdown by Cowboys." The Star Tribune. Nov, 21, 2022.

[lvi] Goessling, Ben. "Vikings Suffer Worst Home Loss in 59 Years in 40-3 Smackdown by Cowboys." The Star Tribune. Nov, 21, 2022.

[lvii] "Rodgers, Packers Route Vikings 41-17, Control Playoff Fate." ESPN.Com. Jan. 1, 2023. Web.

[lviii] "Giants Outlast Vikings 31-24 For First Playoff Win in 11 Years." ESPN.Com. Jan. 15, 2023. Web.

[lix] Seifert, Kevin. "Kirk Cousins: Giants Loss Probably the Toughest of Career Given 13 Wins." ESPN.Com. Jan. 15, 2023.

[lx] Seifert, Kevin. "Kirk Cousins: Giants Loss Probably the Toughest of Career Given 13 Wins." ESPN.Com. Jan. 15, 2023.
[lxi] Nelson, Joe. "Kirk Cousins Focused on Earning Contract Extension from Vikings." Sports Illustrated. May 3, 2023.
[lxii] Kogod, Sarah. "Kirk Cousins' Proposal Story." The Washington Post. Dec. 5, 2013.
[lxiii] Kogod, Sarah. "Kirk Cousins' Proposal Story." The Washington Post. Dec. 5, 2013.
[lxiv] Kogod, Sarah. "Kirk Cousins' Proposal Story." The Washington Post. Dec. 5, 2013.
[lxv] Ragatz, Will. "Vikings QB Kirk Cousins Donates $500,000 to Team's Social Justice Committee." Sports Illustrated. Oct. 13, 2021.

Made in the USA
Las Vegas, NV
14 August 2023

76075688R00066